MAGIC AND PERCEPTION

MAGIC AND PERCEPTION

THE ART AND SCIENCE OF FOOLING THE SENSES

by Bob Friedhoffer
Illustrations by Linda Eisenberg

Franklin Watts
A Division of Grolier Publishing

New York   London   Hong Kong   Sydney
Danbury, Connecticut

Cover photograph copyright ©: Timothy White

Illustrations copyright ©: Linda Eisenberg

Library of Congress Cataloging-in-Publication Data
Friedhoffer, Robert; illustrations by Linda Eisenberg
    Magic and perception : the art and science of fooling the senses / by
Bob Friedhoffer.
        p.   cm.
    Includes bibliographical references and index.
    Summary: Presents step-by-step instructions for a variety of magic
tricks, explaining how the tricks work by affecting people's perceptions.
    ISBN 0-531-11254-3 (lib bdg.) — ISBN 0-531-15803-9 (pbk.)
    1. Conjuring—Juvenile literature. 2. Tricks—Juvenile literature. [1.
Magic tricks.] I. Title.
GV1548.F73 1996
793.8—dc20   95-51214
                                                                  CIP
                                                                   AC

DEDICATION

This book is dedicated to my good friend Dr. Harold "Heshie" Axe, who convinced me that the effectiveness of allergy shots is not just an illusion.

ACKNOWLEDGMENTS

I would like to thank the following people whose help, encouragement, and ideas helped make this book a possibility: Dr. Stephan Baumrin, Mark Setteducati, Richard Crist, Tom "Boom-Boom" Ladshaw, Michael Chaut, Dr. Tom Riedl, Art Kahn, Tim Folger, Melvin Burkhart, Rudy and the crew at Peppermint Park, and last but not least, Annette.

CONTENTS

MAGIC AND PERCEPTION

WHAT IS PERCEPTION?

When I first started doing magic tricks, I thought it was awesome that I could fool people. I could do things they couldn't do. Not only couldn't they do them, they couldn't figure out how to do them.

Being the nosy kind of guy I am, I wanted to know how and why people get fooled. If I knew that, I thought, maybe I'd become a better magician. So I started studying different things, both in school and out—things such as acting, stagecraft, and the history of magic and science.

It dawned on me, after a while, that there are many scientific reasons for why magic fools people. Some of them have to do with laws of physics, which I've discussed at length in some of my other books. Others are based on principles of chemistry and biology, which I've touched on in other books. But quite a few of the reasons have to do with the science of the mind, better known as psychology, and the science of the brain, neurology. These are the areas this book concentrates on.

Right about now you might be wondering, "How can knowing anything about the science of the brain help you fool someone?" The important part of a magical performance, I discovered, is not what you do, but what people think you do. In other words, what counts is how the audience perceives the trick.

So what the heck is perception anyway? The tenth edition of *Merriam Webster's Collegiate Dictionary* gives one definition of the word *perceive* as "to become aware of through the senses." That gives a good general idea of perception, but it doesn't tell the whole story.

To be precise, perception is the interpretation by the brain of information gathered by the five senses—sight, hearing, smell, touch, and taste. The organs that allow us to perceive are our eyes, ears, nose, tongue, and skin. The input to these organs is called stimuli. Once received by our organs, the stimuli is sometimes called *sense data*.

The sense organs convert the sense data into impulses, which are transmitted to our brains by our nervous system. In the brain, the impulses create "sensory states," which the brain interprets based upon our *past experience*.

Relying on past experience helps the brain deal

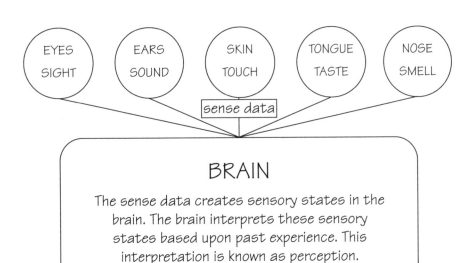

EYES	EARS	SKIN	TONGUE	NOSE
SIGHT	SOUND	TOUCH	TASTE	SMELL

sense data

BRAIN

The sense data creates sensory states in the brain. The brain interprets these sensory states based upon past experience. This interpretation is known as perception.

with the overwhelming amount of sense data that comes in. If we had to approach everything as if for the first time, we'd never get anything done. The interpretations the brain makes are like shortcuts to the information that we really need.

You'll find that many magic tricks take advantage of our reliance on past experience. The interpretation of past experience is called *inference*. Based upon our inferences, we decode sense data to get meaning from it. The entire process from the gathering of sense data by our sense organs to the decoding in the brain is known as perception. We are experiencing perception at every waking instant.

voila

Studying magic tricks can give you a feeling for the difference between the raw sense data and the inferences the brain makes. When you are fooled by a magic trick and then learn the secret behind it, the strange workings of the mind become very apparent.

You will learn that magicians can easily fool people by simply allowing them to perceive only a small portion of what is really going on. The magician artfully produces a false perception in the mind of the spectator by controlling the sense data that the spectator sees, hears, feels, tastes, or smells.

The magician knows from experience the inferences the spectator will make from that sense data. Under normal conditions these inferences would be accurate, but in the world of magic, they can lead people astray.

I have selected the tricks in this book because they are particularly good for helping the reader understand how sense data can be manipulated. I do not pretend to cover all areas of perception and illusions. If you are interested in learning more, read the books in For Further Reading at the back of the book.

practice

PERFORMING MAGIC

Unless you learn to do the tricks yourself and try them out on friends, you will find it difficult to understand how the magician controls perception. There is only one way to learn to do a magic trick well enough to fool someone. You must practice your tricks until you know them backward and forward. This is the first and perhaps most important secret of magic.

Learn both the manipulation

and the patter—the talking part. If you try to perform a trick for your friends before you can do it properly, it may fall flat. And you may be so discouraged that you never try again. So remember that practice is the key to performing magic. If you can, practice in front of a mirror or a video camera so you can see what the audience will see.

Who knows, you might enjoy it so much that you become a professional magician—or a brain scientist!

OPTICAL ILLUSIONS

Most of a magician's bag of tricks rely on deceiving the eyes more than any other sense organ. There's a good reason for that. Humans depend a great deal on sight for their information.

The science of sight is fascinating. I am indebted to Bernard H. Baumrin, a philosopher of science at City University of New York, for providing the following explanation of how sight works—and doesn't work—in people.

Although all mammals have five senses, they tend to rely on some senses more than others. Dogs do more information gathering and interpreting with their noses than we humans do, and certain nocturnal animals do more with their ears than we do. Because we get so much information from our eyes, we are usually more confident in what we see than in what we hear. We learn to distrust the experience of all our senses, but we distrust sight the least. Still, we are often deceived by our sense of sight.

There are two reasons this happens, according

to Professor Baumrin. First, what we are looking at may be too fleeting, too obscured, too new, too odd. Second, our minds have a great deal to do with what we sense.

rabbit

duck

To experience sight deception for yourself, look at the drawings in the margins of this page. Is the figure a duck or a rabbit? Do the square lines mark a pyramid or a square hole? Are the stairs right side up or upside down? Put a pencil in a glass of water and look at it. Is the pencil straight or crooked? These are all examples of *optical illusions,* images that mislead the brain.

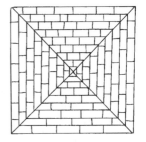

Examples of purely mental deceptions are harder to give because they are nearly impossible to detect. Nothing we see—not the light, the shape, nor the color—reaches the brain in the form that it strikes the eye. Patterns of light hit the eye, but a series of electrical impulses goes to the brain, where they are reconstructed and interpreted as an image.

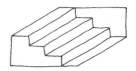

But most of the information that hits the eye goes no further. The little bit of information that is processed produces the image. So we see only what our brains are able to interpret.

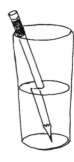

For example, we don't see anything in the ultraviolet or infrared ends of the light spectrum. We see only what is called visible light, the wavelengths in the middle of the electromagnetic spectrum. If things go by too quickly, we will see even less—blurs or perhaps nothing. As magicians say, the hand is quicker than the eye. What they really mean is the hand is sneakier than the mind, for the mind has the ultimate control over what we see.

We will explore the sight deceptions associated with movement in later chapters. This chapter concentrates on optical illusions, deceptions that come from motionless images.

RELATIVE SIZE PERCEPTION

Sometimes it is very difficult to tell the size of an object because of preconceived ideas. A good example can be found in a 1960's TV show called "Laugh-In." One of the regular segments featured a child named Edith Ann, who was played by the adult actress Lily Tomlin.

It was not just Ms. Tomlin's acting talent that made Edith Ann appear to be a little girl. It was also that she

sat in a humongous, oversized rocking chair. It was built to such a scale that it dwarfed an ordinary adult.

Our past experience teaches us the size of a child or an adult compared with that of a chair. When viewers saw Edith Ann in the chair, they assumed she was a small child in a chair of normal size instead of an adult in a giant chair.

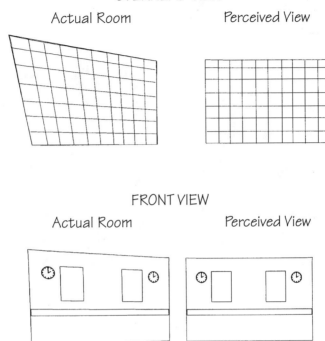

OVERHEAD VIEW

Actual Room   Perceived View

FRONT VIEW

Actual Room   Perceived View

FIGURE 1

Many science museums around the country use the same idea to create rooms that make people look huge or small, depending on where they stand. One such room at the New York Hall of Science in Flushing Meadows, Queens, has walls and a floor with skewed dimensions, as shown in Figure 1. The tiles on the floor and the decorations on the walls are also skewed to give the impression that it is a normal rectangular room. As a result, it appears that people on the shortened side of the room are big and people on the other side are small, as shown in the photographs on the facing page.

You can see another version of the phenomenon

That's me, Bob, in a room at the New York Hall of Science. The giant on the right is a friend, Tim Folger.

When we switch places, I double in size, but Tim's feeling small.

by looking at the top hat in Figure 2. Which distance is longer—the distance from brim to brim, A to B, or the height of the top hat, C to D?

Measure each with a ruler to find the answer. Can you see how the width of an object influences our perception of its height?

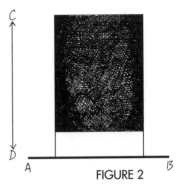

FIGURE 2

Next, I will teach you an actual trick based on our faulty perception of relative size.

The Incredible Shrinking Banana

Effect:
A banana grows and shrinks at your command.

Props:
• Two bananas identical in size.

Routine:
Place one banana on a table. Hold the second banana directly above the first and show the spectators that they are identical in size.

Now pretend to stretch the banana in your hands and place it on the table so that it is against the other banana's outward-curving side, as shown in Figure 3. Align the stem ends of the bananas. It will appear that the second banana is larger.

Pick up the second banana and pretend to push it

FIGURE 3

back to its original size. Place it on the table, this time on the other side of the first banana, aligning the stem ends once again. Now the second banana will appear to be smaller than the first banana.

Pick up the second banana and "stretch" it one more time. This time place it directly atop the banana on the table. They will once again appear to be the same size.

At this point you might want to offer one of the bananas to a spectator. Hopefully, the person will eat it and destroy all evidence of how the trick works. Even if the spectator doesn't eat the banana, eat yours to prevent her from figuring out the trick.

You will know you've mastered this trick when a member of your audience goes into a supermarket and asks for one of those variable-size bananas!

The Perception:

I would venture to guess that this trick was invented when a magician looked at some bananas in a supermarket and realized the illusion that curved objects create. Most magicians perform this trick with flat sticks shaped something like boomerangs, always of the same size. Richard E. Churchill's book *How to Make Optical Illusion Tricks and Toys* shows how to easily make a pair of cardboard boomerangs.

Figure 4 shows two boomerangs of identical

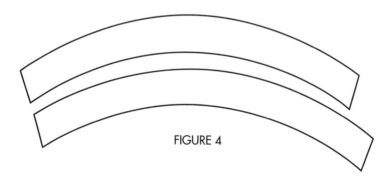

FIGURE 4

size. It may appear that the one on bottom is larger, but it is the same size as the other one. In any arced object of significant width, the side of the object curving outward is always longer than the side curving inward. So when the inward curve of one object is placed next to the outward curve of another object, the object with the outward curve in contact appears longer.

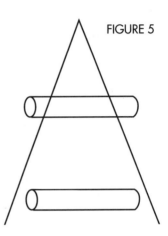

FIGURE 5

A similar effect can be seen in Figure 5. Which cylinder is longer? The upper or the lower?

Believe it or not, they are both the same size.

DEPTH PERCEPTION

Is something close or far away? It is often quite difficult to judge where an object is in relation to us.

It is easier to judge distance when one object partially blocks the view of another object. We know that the object that is blocked is the one that's farther away.

A second way we judge distance is by the size of the object. We know from experience that an object appears larger if it's closer and smaller if it is farther away.

Thirdly, we rely on our built-in depth perception, which works in part simply because we have two eyes. Located in different places on the head, each eye sees a slightly different version of the same scene. In the process of combining these images, the brain receives information about the distance of the objects in the scene.

Vision that involves the combining of images from two eyes is called *stereoscopic vision*. Here's a quick experiment that proves that having two eyes helps us gauge distances, at least up to about 40 inches (100 cm).

Materials:
- A yardstick or meter stick.

Procedure:
Hold one end of the yard-stick under your chin with your left hand. The other end should be pointing straight out from your body, as shown in Figure 6. Extend your right hand alongside the yardstick at the same height. Your hand should be about 8 inches (20 cm) to the right of the yardstick. Now point toward the stick with your right index finger.

FIGURE 6

Close your left eye. Look at the 18-inch (45-cm) mark on the stick with your right eye. Keeping your right hand 8 inches from the stick, try to align your index finger with the 18-inch mark. When you think you have done so, move your index finger leftward until it touches the stick. Open your left eye and see whether you touched the 18-inch mark. Try it again with a few different marks on the stick.

Next, do the experiment with both eyes open. Did you have better luck hitting the marks? Keep a record of your hits and misses on a chart like the following:

DISTANCE	1 EYE	2 EYES	INCHES OFF

This experiment should give you a feel for how stereoscopic vision works. We will take advantage of this phenomenon in the magic trick called "The X-Ray Tube" on p. 79.

PERSPECTIVE

Look at the jumble of lines in Figure 7. What do you see? Believe it or not, there are three messages hidden in the

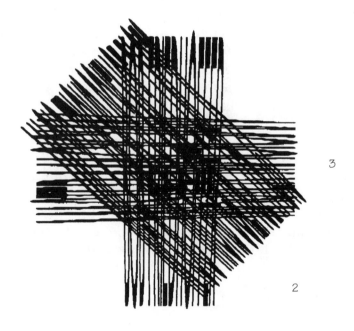

3

2

1 FIGURE 7

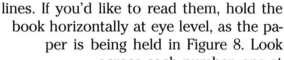

lines. If you'd like to read them, hold the book horizontally at eye level, as the paper is being held in Figure 8. Look across each number, one at a time. The messages should now be quite readable.

FIGURE 8

These messages were made with the help of a computer drawing program. It stretched the words of the messages vertically and then widened the tops of the words just a touch. After that, each message was rotated to the position you see it in now.

The reason the words were widened at the top is to counter an illusion of perspective. Have you ever stood on a long straight stretch of railroad track and looked along its length? Perspective creates the illusion that the rails move closer together until they join in a "V." The rails also appear to be shorter, an effect called foreshortening.

These effects make it possible to read the messages in Figure 7. As you tilt the page toward your eye, the message becomes readable because your perspective has changed. At one point, the letters are shortened until they appear normal.

If the words were not widened, they would be more difficult, if not impossible, to read.* Because of the "V" effect, the tops would appear to be squished together. Note that this effect also causes the other messages to blur into a gray blob.

The author wishes to thank Richard Crist for pointing out the benefit of widening the top portions.

The messages read:

1. Bob Friedhoffer
2. Magic Tricks, Science Facts
3. Master Magician

OPTICS

Melvin Burkhart, a well-known sideshow magician, made a comment about visual illusions in 1992. He said, "They say that seeing is believing. If you can see me you can believe me. What you see ain't always what you're looking at—in case you wasn't watching." What he was saying was that people often make the mistake of believing that their eyesight is perfect and nothing can fool it.

Here's a strange trick that proves Melvin's point.

The Confusing Arrow

Effect:

An arrow printed on a piece of paper mysteriously changes the direction it is pointing.

Props:

• A glass filled with water. The sides of the glass should be clear and smooth with no decorations.

• A line of arrows printed on a strip of paper as shown in Figure 9. You can make the strip by Xeroxing Fig. 9, enlarging it about 3

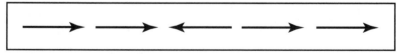

FIGURE 9

times. Each arrow should be a little shorter than the width of your glass.

Routine:

Place the glass of water on the table. Have your spectator sit in front of the glass. You sit across from your spectator.

Hold the strip of paper behind the glass as shown in Figure 10. The center arrow should be directly behind the glass so that the spectator sees it when looking through the water. The center arrow will appear to be pointing in the same direction as the other arrows, as shown in Figure 11.

When you snap your fingers and pull the strip of paper from behind the glass, it will look as if the arrow has changed direction.

FIGURE 10

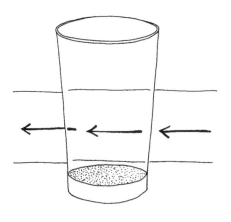

FIGURE 11

The Perception:

Most people think they can't be fooled because they're too darn clever. They believe their eyes all of the time. This trick proves that your eyes can be tricked pretty easily by something as simple as a glass of water.

The principle operating here comes from the science of optics. When you fill the glass with water, you are creating a lens. The lens reverses the image from left to right. What is normally on the left appears to be on the right. What is normally on the right appears to be on the left. Whatever is in the middle, stays in the middle. The top and bottom also stay where they are. In other words, the right and left sides appear to switch places.

Figure 12 shows exactly what happens to the light traveling from the arrow to the eyes. The glass alters the direction of the light coming to the eye, creating a false, inverted image of the arrow. This is how a convex lens works.

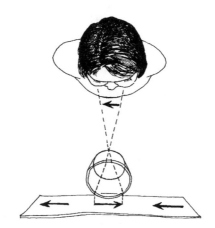

FIGURE 12

INVISIBILITY

Under the proper circumstances an object may become invisible. In nature many animals become invisible by virtue of pelts, scales, or skin that act as camouflage. A zebra's stripes, a leopard's spots, a frog's mottled skin help these animals blend into the background so that predators or prey can't see them.

Armed forces around the world have adopted similar camouflage in the clothing they wear during battle.

To become invisible, a camouflaged object must be motionless against the proper background. Once it is in motion, it becomes much easier to identify. For years, this problem has bedeviled magicians who do tricks with thread.

Magicians use thread or long strands of hair to animate, suspend, or levitate objects. One problem with thread in general is that the thinner the thread, the weaker it is. It's difficult to see a very thin thread, but if it's too thin it will break easily. The thicker and stronger the thread, the easier it is to see.

The color of the thread also comes into play. For many years, magicians used only black thread because they assumed it is the least visible color. However, black thread can be visible against light backgrounds.

Some magicians came up with the idea that it would be more difficult to see a purple thread. Others said that dying the thread different dark colors every few inches was the answer. An audience member might see an inch or two of it but then lose it again.

One way to dye thread to get the multicolor effect is to mark a spool of white cotton thread with dark marker pens. It can be done with the thread still on the spool by making alternating stripes of color around the spool. When the thread is unwound, it will have short lengths of different colors.

Other magicians tried using nylon monofilament fishing line, which is quite strong and colorless. The problem with monofilament line, however, is that it's very shiny. The audience may not see the thread, but they may easily see the reflection of light from it.

All of these thread ideas work to some degree,

but they depend upon dark stage lighting. The darker the stage, the less visible the thread. Unfortunately, the trick is also less visible on a dark stage.

Finally someone came up with the great idea of changing the background behind the thread. If the background is a solid color, it's easier to see a long straight thread. If the background is mottled or multicolored, it is much harder for the human eye to see the thread.

The next trick makes use of the principle of masking with a varicolored background. I've seen it performed on the streets in many cities around the world.

The Dancing Cardboard Man

Effect:
At your command, a small cutout cardboard figure dances in place.

Props:
> • Thin monofilament thread. Sewing sections of department stores have a very thin thread called "invisible thread." In reality, it is invisible only when the conditions are perfect.

> • A multicolored cotton thread. Make it by marking a spool of white thread as specified in the introduction to this trick, except the colors should be a little on the light side.

> • A dancing cardboard figure about 5 inches (13 cm) high, like the one in Figure 13. You can make one by reproducing the illustration on a copy machine and cutting it out of

FIGURE 13

the copy. Then trace it onto cardboard and cut it out. Do *not* cut the figure out of this book!

• Make the legs from thin yarn or thick string and glue the feet to it. Notice how the figure's ear lobes are separated from the head. The ear lobes should be bent backward just a little bit. Decorate the figure in bright colors.

Setup:

You must have an assistant to work the thread. No one but you should know you are using an assistant.

It is best to perform this trick on an overcast day or in a shadowed area on a bright day. The background should be a neutral, mottled color—not too light or too dark. A stone or granite wall is perfect. A background of greenery such as a line of hedges also works well.

In front of the backdrop, you must stretch the thread horizontally about 4 to 5 inches (10 to 13 cm) above the ground. One end of the thread must be anchored to something, such as a lamppost, drainpipe, or even your schoolbag. The thread should be about 4 to 6 inches (10 to 15 cm) in front of the background.

Your assistant should hold the other end of the thread about 6 to 10 feet (2 to 3 m) away from the anchored end. To keep the audience from seeing what she's doing, have her drape a jacket over her hand or put her hand inside a jacket pocket.

The thread should sag slightly from your assistant's hand to the anchor point. Hang the figure on the thread by placing the earlobes behind the thread and the rest of the figure in front of it. Your assistant should adjust her stance so that the cutout's feet just brush the ground.

Routine:

Start out by saying, "Ladies and Gentlemen, watch carefully as my colorful little assistant performs for your viewing pleasure. He dances, walks, jogs, and boogies."

Start to hum a tune, play a kazoo, or turn on a tape deck. Your undercover assistant should gently tug on the thread in time to the music. The cutout should now also be moving in time to the music. When there is a break in the music, your assistant should let the string go slack so that the cutout falls to the floor.

After a moment, snap your fingers about 6 inches (15 cm) over the cutout. With a jerk, your assistant should make it jump up off the ground into your waiting fingertips. Grasp the cutout and pull straight up, disengaging it from the string. At that point, your assistant should slacken the string so that it falls to the ground and lies there unseen by your audience.

The Perception:

This trick is based, of course, on the principle of invisibility. The thread cannot be seen against your background, so it looks to spectators as if the cardboard man has a life of his own.

Since the seventies, it has become the fashion among some magicians to perform against a well-lit backdrop of shiny metallic foil. Because there are reflections of all sorts bouncing from the background, the audience's eyes and brains are overwhelmed with processing a lot of random information. As a result, many small objects become invisible. The reflections tend to break up the audience's view of the edges of all objects. Therefore, if a neutral wire or thread is relatively motionless against this type of background, it is usually invisible to the audience.

SLEIGHT
OF HAND

O ne basic principle of magic is directly related to perception. It is responsible for much of the sleight of hand that takes place on a magician's stage. In case you're unfamiliar with the term, sleight of hand is any sneaky move that is not seen by the audience.

This chapter covers an underlying principle of sleight of hand that might be stated as, "a small movement is usually masked by a large movement." What does this mean?

Try this experiment. Stand in front of a mirror with one arm out to the side and wave it up and down. What do you see? Now as you wave your arm up and down, wiggle your fingers. What do you see?

Notice how the wiggling of your fingers is hidden by the movement of your arm. The movement of your flailing arm is so large that it is quite difficult to make out the small movement of your fingers. In other words, you don't perceive the small details because you are distracted by the overall motion.

There are many tricks that make use of this principle. Here are two of them that will teach you how it works. Many other tricks in the book also rely on it to some degree.

PADDLE TRICKS

Paddle tricks of all sorts make use of the "small-movement-masked-by-a-large-movement principle" to fool the audience. Many paddle tricks have been devised over the years, and some of them are sold in stores.

Here's one you can do at home, in a restaurant, or in a cafeteria with a minimum amount of practice using articles that are easy to find.

The Vanishing Paper Squares

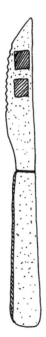

Effect:
Little squares of paper stuck to a knife blade vanish and appear in a most perplexing manner.

Props:
• A dull butter knife.

• Three 1/4-inch (1/2-cm) square pieces of paper.

Setup:
The squares must be stuck to the blade of the butter knife, two on one side, one on the other. Make them stick by dipping them into a glass of water, then laying them flat on the knife's blade, as shown in Figures 14a and 14b.

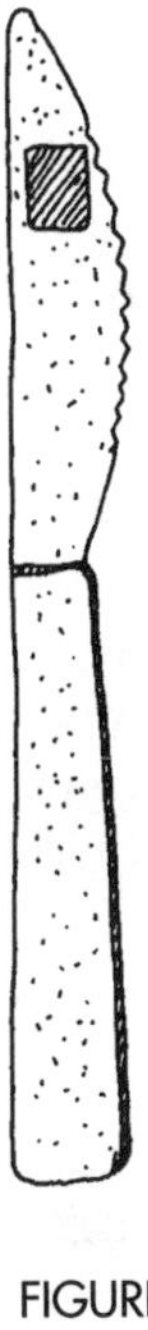

FIGURE 14 a

FIGURE 14 b

Moves to Practice:

Move 1:

Hold the knife handle with the fingers of your right hand, as shown in Figure 15. The thumb and pinkie are above the blade, and the 1st, 2nd, and 3rd fingers are on the underside.

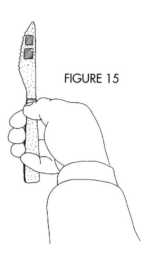

FIGURE 15

The back of the hand should be parallel to the floor. The side of the blade with two squares on it should face upward.

Flip the blade one-half-turn by moving the thumb sideways toward your fingertips. If you have done this properly, the side with one square should face upward, as shown in Figure 16. The pinkie acts as a brace; it doesn't move. Using it as a brace makes the trick easier to perform.

Now move the thumb back to its original position, reversing the blade. The two squares should be visible once again. Practice this move until you can do it smoothly and rapidly.

Move 2:

Turn your hand over so that the palm faces the floor. The knife should flip lengthwise this time, and the side with

FIGURE 16

one square should now be showing. Turn your hand back to the
starting position.

FIGURE 17

Move 3:

Now for the part where you fool
people. Begin in the original position, with two squares facing upward on the blade, as in Figure 17.

Turn your hand over so that
the palm is down, as if to show
your spectators the other side of
the blade. At the same time,
move your thumb sideways,
causing the blade to make a one-
half-turn, just as you did before.

Two squares should be showing, as in Figure 18.

Hold your hand still for
a beat or two. Then return it
to the palm-up position,
while pulling your thumb
back in the other direction
to make another half-turn.
The knife should now be
back in its original position.

FIGURE 18

You act as if you
are turning your hand
over to show both sides of the blade, but in reality,
you are showing only one side of the blade because
you turned your hand and the blade at the same
time. The audience will think they saw both sides of
the knife blade. To magicians, this is known as "the
paddle move."

Practice until you can do the paddle move

smoothly in both directions. Once you've mastered it, you're ready to perform the trick.

Routine:

Hold the knife so that the side with two squares is showing, with the back of your hand toward the floor.

Do the paddle move so that the spectators think they have seen both sides of the blade.

Now say, "I have four squares of paper on this knife blade. I am going to remove two squares."

Your left hand should be palm up, with the left thumb higher than the other fingers.

Move the blade toward the left hand. Just as the left thumb starts to cover one of the squares, turn the knife over with your right thumb (move 1).

The left thumb should now appear to be resting on one of the squares. In reality, the square is on the bottom side of the blade, and your thumb is resting directly on the blade. The fingers of the left hand should be on the bottom of the blade.

Pretend to remove the square under your left thumb (the square that is not there), as well as the square on the other side directly underneath the thumb. Do not remove anything, just pretend. Fold your left hand into a loose fist as if you were holding two squares.

Turn your right hand over a few times, back and forth, doing the paddle move (move 3). Move your thumb back and forth at the appropriate times so that your spectators don't see that you are flipping the knife sideways as you rotate it end to end. It should appear to them that there is only one square on each side of the blade.

Now say, "Watch! I will throw the pieces of paper back onto the knife blade."

Pretend to throw the paper back onto the blade

by flinging your left hand and right hand toward each other. Just as you open your left hand, flip the blade with your right thumb. The side with two squares should now be visible. If you practice this move enough, it will look as if you simply tossed the squares back onto the blade.

Now turn your hand over and back once or twice in the paddle move. The audience will be convinced that both sides once again have two squares.

The Perception:
The large movement of turning your hand over and back masks the smaller movement of your thumb flipping the knife from side-to-side. The audience will be so caught up with move 2 that they will not notice move 1.

Another factor operating in this trick is the audience's past experience, a principle that is explored in greater depth in Chapter 4. We know from past experience that when someone holding an object in a hand turns the hand over, the other side of the object comes into view. We expect it to happen. It is an inference we make.

The paddle move manipulates the sense data going to the spectator's eye in such a way that people believe they have seen both sides of the knife blade.

If you wish to buy a paddle trick in a magic store, here are the names of three I recommend:

• Rabbit In the Hat Paddle®

• Hot Rod®

• Slip Off Spots®

Fly Away, Jack!

In the 1872 book *Hanky Panky, a Book of Easy and Difficult Conjuring Tricks,* W. H. Cremer describes a trick using the "small-movement-masked-by-a-large-movement principle." The following is an updated version, with an adaptation of the patter found in *Hanky Panky.*

This is a wonderful trick for little kids. Don't pass it by simply because it seems too easy or babyish.

Effect:

Two paper squares vanish from your fingertips and reappear in a mysterious manner.

Props:

- Two 1/4-inch (1/2 cm) squares of paper.

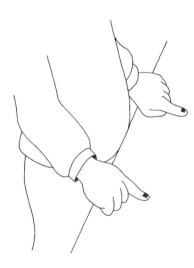

FIGURE 19

Setup:

Moisten both pieces of paper with water. Place one piece on the nail of each index finger, making sure the squares stick.

Keep your index fingers extended while curling the rest of the fingers of each hand into a fist. Rest your index fingers about 6 inches (15 cm) apart from each other on a table's edge, as shown in Figure 19.

Routine:

You say:

"Two little birds sat
on the sill,
One named Jack, the
other Jill.
Fly away, Jack!"

Then raise your right
fist to a position
straight up, just above
your head, and bring
it back down toward
the tabletop. As your
hand reaches the top

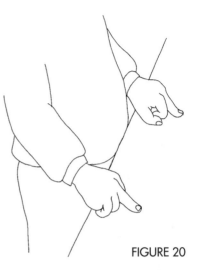

FIGURE 20

of your head, quickly tuck your index finger, with the
paper square, into your fist and extend your middle
finger. It might help to hold the index finger in place
with your right thumb.

Bring your middle finger down onto the tabletop. The spectators will think the paper has vanished. If you practice this move, people will not realize you have switched fingers.

Next say, "Fly away, Jill!" As you say it, raise your
left hand in the air and quickly switch the left middle
finger for the index finger. Your hands should now appear as in Figure 20.

The spectators will think the two middle fingers
are the two index fingers with the paper squares
missing.

Next say, "Come back, Jack!" Raise your right
hand again. Extend the index finger with the paper
square still on it and curl the middle finger into the
fist. Bring the index finger back to the tabletop.

Follow this up with, "Come back, Jill!" Raise your
left hand and switch fingers as you did with the

right hand and bring the index finger back to the tabletop.

Now it will seem to the spectators that the "two little birds," the paper squares, have come back.

The Perception:
Because the large arm movement concealed the small finger movement, the spectators will not realize that you showed different fingers each time. They will think they have always seen two index fingers.

The Ethereal Corks

Effect:
One cork penetrates another as though it wasn't there.

Props:
- Two cylindrical corks about 3/4 inches (2 cm) in diameter by 2 inches (5 cm) long.

Setup:
Lay one cork on its side on a tabletop. Hold the other cork by its ends with the thumb and first finger of the left hand. Then place it across the cork on the table, but don't release the cork. The corks should form an "X."

Insert the thumb of the right hand down into the space between the thumb and first finger of the left hand, and grasp the ends of the cork on the table with the right thumb and forefinger.

Lift both hands up. The corks should now be locked in place with the fingertips, as shown in Figure 21. Unless you let go of a cork, you cannot separate them.

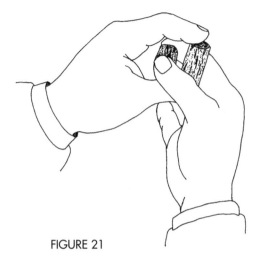

FIGURE 21

Routine:

Start out by showing your spectators the corks, making it quite clear that they are locked in place. It should be obvious that there are only two ways they could be separated: 1) by letting go of one of the corks, or 2) by making one magically penetrate the other.

To create the illusion of the second possibility, simply raise your hands and free the corks, with the help of some hidden movements.

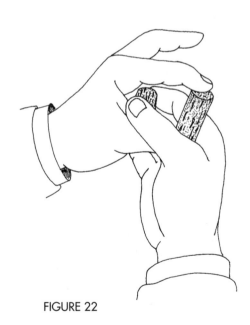

FIGURE 22

Moves to Practice:

This trick requires a lot of practice in front of a mirror. Much like the previous tricks, it consists of one small movement plus two large movements that will take place simultaneously. Keep in mind that the goal is to separate your hands.

Small Move:
Push the cork in your left hand into the crotch between the

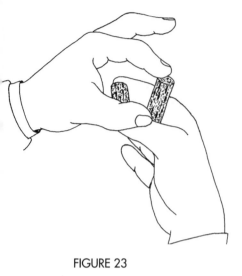

FIGURE 23

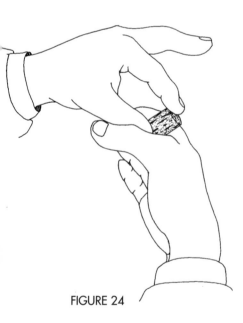

FIGURE 24

right thumb and first finger. The thumb end of the left-hand cork should be as high in the crotch as possible, as shown in Figure 22. Squeeze the crotch of your right hand around the left-hand cork.

With your left index finger, push the top of the left-hand cork toward your right wrist so that the cork pivots on the edge of your right hand. As you do this, release the left thumb from the bottom of the cork.

Bring your left thumb around the right thumb, as shown in Figure 23. Once again grasp the bottom of the cork, as in Figure 24. Now you should be holding both corks between thumb and forefinger as before, but they should be free of each other (Figure 25).

Large Moves:
Hold your hands in front of your chest, displaying both corks to the spectators. Move your hands upward and to the right, stopping at shoulder height to the right of your body.

During this move, rotate the back of the left hand so that it faces the spectator at the end of the move. As the left hand rotates, perform the small move. When the left hand reconnects with the bottom of the cork, separate your hands.

The Perception:
Once mastered, this trick will totally bamboozle your audience because they will not be able to see the small movements of your left thumb and forefinger. By rotating the back of your left hand, you are obstructing the view of the sneaky thumb, as well as distracting from the small movements of your fingers.

As in most tricks that depend upon sleight of hand, the smoothness of the movements is more important than their speed.

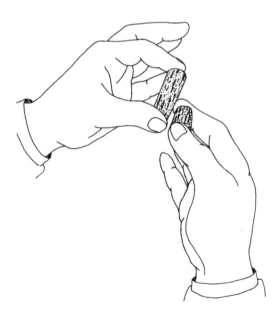

FIGURE 25

PAST EXPERIENCE

As you learned in the first chapter, just about every magic trick depends to some degree on people making faulty inferences based on previous experiences they've had. The experiences may have occurred as early as childhood, or the magician may have orchestrated the experience only a few moments before.

The tricks in this chapter demonstrate particularly well the ways that magicians make use of past experience.

Find The Queen

Effect:
You display five cards in a row with a queen in the center. After you turn them over, a spectator chooses the wrong location of the queen.

Props:
- 5 playing cards. One of them should be a red queen and the rest, black number cards.

- Invisible cellophane tape.

- A paper clip.

- A no. 10 envelope.

Setup:
Place the cards on a table, face down, one overlapping the next by about an inch (2 cm). The red queen should be in the middle. Neatly tape the cards together. Turn the cards over and tape them on the face side, too.

You now have a permanent prop. Store it in the no. 10 envelope, along with the paper clip.

Routine:
Take the spread of cards from the envelope and show it to your audience. As you show it to them, say, "These are five playing cards that I have taped together."

Take the paper clip from the envelope and hand it to someone in the audience. Say, "I'd like you to clip this to the top edge of the queen so that it is on her face." Your helper should have no problem doing as you request. (Figure 26).

Now remove the paper clip from the queen and turn the spread of cards over. Make mystical gestures over the cards and tell your friend, "With my magical powers, I have made it impossible for you to put the paper clip on the face of the

FIGURE 26

queen from the back of the cards."

Let your friend try clipping the queen, as shown in Figure 27. When you turn the spread over, your audience will be surprised to see that the clip is on the card next to the queen and has totally missed her face, as in Figure 28.

The Perception:
When the cards are viewed from the front, it is no big deal to put the clip on the queen. When they are turned over, it's another story.

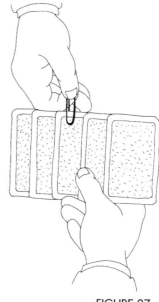

FIGURE 27

Realizing that the queen is still the middle card when viewed from the rear, most people assume they can clip the queen in the same way they did before. They rely on their experience from just a few moments before.

FIGURE 28

What they don't realize—simply because they don't take the time to think about it—is that from the front, the adjacent card overlaps the queen at that point. So sliding a clip over the middle card, as in Figure 27, misses the queen's face completely.

The Changing Spot Card

Effect:
A flat piece of cardboard with two sides is shown to have four sides.

Prop:
    • A piece of cardboard, 4 inches by 6 inches (10 cm by 15 cm). One side should have two spots and the other side five spots arranged

FIGURE 29a

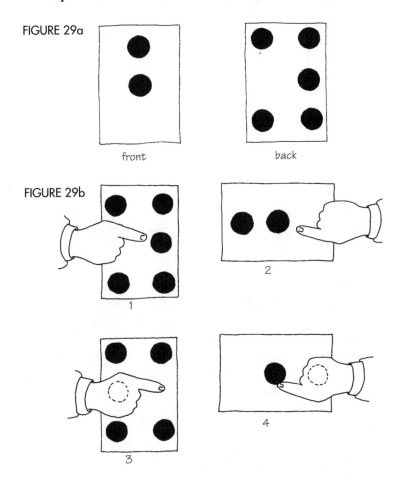

front   back

FIGURE 29b

1

2

3

4

as in Figure 29a. Make the spots with paint or a marker pen.

Routine:

Hold the card with the five-spot side facing the audience, partially covering the empty space with your hand, as shown in the first step of Figure 29b. Say, "This card is weird. It has four sides. Let me show them to you."

As you turn the card over with your other hand, you must cover the empty space on the other side of the card, as shown in the second step of Figure 29b. Turn the card a total of three times in the sequence shown, saying, "There's a six on one side, a three on the other side, a four on the other side, and an ace on the fourth side." With each turn, your hand covers either a spot or a place you want the audience to believe a spot exists.

To the audience, it will appear that you are telling the truth. They will have to conclude that the card has four sides. Before doing this trick, practice moving your hand smoothly to the appropriate positions in the sequence shown in the illustration.

The Perception:

This trick relies heavily on past experience with playing cards. In fact, if it is performed for a young kid who is not familiar with cards, the trick will not work.

Because most people are very familiar with the symmetrical spots on playing cards, they will assume that your spots follow the same pattern. Your verbal cues also contribute to the illusion that they are seeing a six, a three, a four, and an ace. Their past experience is so ingrained that they may believe they actually see the spots and won't even notice your hand in the places they should be.

The Bent Fork

This trick is meant to be performed as a one-on-one trick.

Effect:

You show an ordinary fork to your audience of one. You gently massage the tines with your fingers, instantly bending a tine at a 45-degree angle.

Props:

• Pliers.

• An inexpensive metal fork, such as the kind used in cafeterias.

FIGURE 30

Setup:

With the pliers, carefully bend one tine of the fork to the side at something close to a 45-degree angle, as shown in Figure 30. The tine should remain in the same plane as the other tines. Put your special fork into a hiding place such as your bookbag.

Routine:

Take the fork from its hiding place. As you remove it, place your thumb over the bent tine. If you handle it casually and don't make a big deal about it, no one will suspect that it is anything but a regular fork.

With the fork in your left hand, hold your right hand at your spectator's eye level, palm down. Keeping your left thumb over the bent tine, move the

FIGURE 31

FIGURE 32

FIGURE 33

fork to your right hand and grasp its handle with your right thumb and forefinger. The bent tine should be on the side away from the spectator's view. You can now release your left thumb.

The fork should be held so that the edge of the fork is the only thing visible to the spectator, in the position shown in Figure 31. The bent tine is out of sight behind the straight tines.

Slowly rotate your right hand so that the fork is now perpendicular to the floor, as shown in Figure 32. The bent tine should still be hidden behind the others.

With the index finger of your left hand, slowly stroke the gap between the bent and the straight tine. After stroking it for five or six seconds, allow the fork to slowly rotate toward the spectator, as shown in Figure 33. If you do it slowly enough and continue stroking, the gap will appear to grow larger a little bit at a time.

The Perception:

People see forks and other cutlery every day. They assume your fork is just like all the other forks they've had experience with so they don't look at it closely. As long as you handle it casually, they have no reason to suspect that the fork is gimmicked in any way.

The audience sees you hold the fork in a number of different positions—first by the tines, then by the handle. In a subtle way, this proves to them that they are seeing an ordinary fork. Because they assume it's ordinary, they believe you must have done something extraordinary to make the tine bend.

Another important facet of this trick is that you control your spectator's view of the fork. You hide the bent tine until you want to be seen. Then you give the illusion of bending as you stroke the tine by rotating the fork slowly. This takes advantage of the fact that when viewed at an angle, the bend appears to be smaller than it really is. As you rotate the fork, the angle decreases and the bend seems to increase.

OBJECTS IN MOTION

Sometimes we see motion where it doesn't exist. For instance, if you watch a TV show and see a car speeding down the road, is there a little car moving around the inside of your TV set? Of course not; it's just an electronic illusion.

Magicians can sometimes make a motionless object appear to be moving, and they don't have to use electronics to do it. They use visual cues and inference instead. You can do it too in the following trick. You must first construct a magic wand, but it will be well worth the effort. You can have a good time with this one.

The Wand Through the Head

Effect:
You push a magic wand into a spectator's head and then withdraw it. The spectator is none the worse for the effort.

FIGURE 34

Props:
To make a magic wand, gather the following materials:

- 1/2 inch (1.2 cm) wooden dowel, 12 inches (30 cm) long.

- Flat black paint.

- Flat white paint.

- Sheet of white typing paper.

- Cellophane tape.

FIGURE 35

First, paint the dowel black. Then paint 1 inch (2.5 cm) of the dowel at each end white, as shown in Figure 34. Allow the paint to dry thoroughly.

Cut a strip of typing paper 1 inch wide and 2 inches long. Wrap the strip around the wand, making a ring, or loop, 1 inch wide. Tape it closed.

If made properly, the ring should snugly cover one white painted wand tip. In addition, it should slide up and down the wand with little effort, as in Figure 35.

Routine:

This trick can stand on its own, but it is better to include it as part of a routine in which you have a spectator already on the stage.

The spectator may be seated or standing, depending upon who's taller. If he is the same height or taller than you, the spectator should be seated.

Hold the magic wand in your right hand, grasping the paper-covered tip with thumb and forefinger. Say, "Here is a solid magic wand." The audience might think you're lying, so knock the wand against a table's edge to dispel all doubt from their minds.

Step toward the volunteer's right rear side and say, "Are you feeling O.K.?"

Whatever the answer say, "Let's check."

Curl your left hand into a loose fist and place the fist against the volunteer's right temple, with the pinkie touching his temple and the thumb and forefinger toward your right.

Gently place the paperless end of the wand into your left fist and grasp it. The tip of the wand should rest on your pinkie; don't let the end of the wand actually touch the spectator's head.

The back of your right hand, which is gripping the end of the wand, should be toward the audience.

Now say, "Don't move! I know what I'm doing. I once saw a doctor do this on a TV show."

Slowly move your right hand halfway down the length of the wand, pushing the paper ring as

FIGURE 36

you go, as shown in Figure 36. Your right fingertips should be grasping the paper ring. As you move down the wand, make sure your right forearm hides from the audience the portion of the wand that the tip has slid across.

If done properly, it will look as though the wand has slid right into his head. You might ask, "Does it hurt much?"

After a moment, slowly pull the ring back to its original position at the wand's tip. Withdraw it from your left fist.

Look at the end of the wand and say, "Looks like you're a quart low," as if you have just checked the oil in a car.

You may then put the wand down or even use it for another trick. If you do use it for another trick, first remove the paper ring so that no one will have any idea how you performed the trick.

The Perception:

To the audience, this feat looks absolutely impossible. But because of prior experience, the audience cannot help thinking that the wand is moving into the volunteer's head.

Having seen the wand moving around before you do the "insertion," they get used to seeing the white tips moving with it. When the brain gets an image of what looks like a white tip sliding, it automatically assumes the whole wand is sliding too. The brain has no choice but to conclude that the wand is entering the volunteer's head.

The audience's past experience with moving objects in general over their lives also comes into play. They have learned that when they see a small portion of an object move, the entire object moves with it. It is so ingrained that most people never think about it.

Dime to Quarter

This trick appeared in J. B. Bobo's *Modern Coin Magic* in 1952, but it's been around a lot longer than that.

Effect:

You change a dime into a quarter, with no small, sneaky moves of any kind.

Props:

- A dime.

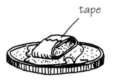

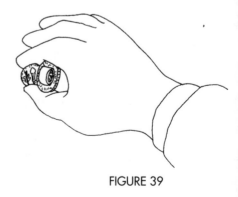

- A quarter.

FIGURE 37

- A piece of cellophane tape formed into a ring about the size of a cigar band. The sticky side should be out.

Setup:

Place the cellophane tape ring on the back, or tails, side of the quarter, as shown in Figure 37. Hold the dime by its edges with the index finger and thumb of the right hand.

If you turn your right hand so that the palm is facing you, you should see the face of the dime, as shown

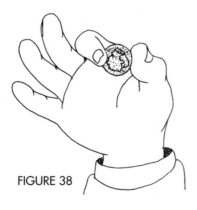

FIGURE 38

FIGURE 39

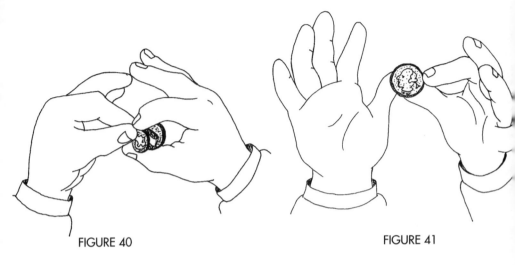

FIGURE 40   FIGURE 41

in Figure 38. Now hold the quarter behind the dime as shown in Figure 39 at an angle of 90° to the dime.

Routine:
Display the coins in the setup position to your spectators. They should see only the dime. The dime blocks the front edge of the quarter while your forefinger and thumb hide the top and bottom edges. No one should suspect that there is anything except a dime in your hand since you are holding it so openly and plainly at your fingertips.

With the left thumb, push the dime down onto the sticky tape side of the quarter, as in Figure 40. At the same time, put your left index finger on the other side of the quarter. Squeezing the dime and quarter so that they stick together, take the two coins between the left thumb and index finger. The index finger should be on the quarter, the thumb on the dime.

Turn your left hand so that the face of the quarter can be seen by your spectators, as shown in

Figure 41. The dime, now stuck to the quarter, should be hidden behind it.

Display the face of the quarter for a moment. Then drop it, tails side down, onto the palm of your right hand. Since they are taped together, the two coins should not separate and there should be no clinking sound. By showing the audience the quarter so fairly and dropping it, you can be sure that no one will suspect that a coin is hidden on the back side.

The Perception:

Since a dime is so small, we all know it is impossible to hide anything as large as a quarter behind one. This comes from past experience. Most people will simply not think about the possibility that the flesh of your fingers could be hiding a quarter.

Surprisingly enough, you can hide even a coin as large as a 50-cent piece behind a dime. Try turning a dime into a half dollar if you have one.

Another factor that enhances the perception you are trying to create is the way you hold the dime. By holding it in a natural position, you give the impression that there is nothing else in your hand. The power of "acting natural" in magic is explored further in the next chapter.

NATURAL
MOVES

I f magicians are to fool anyone, it is vital that they give no clue to their deception. Magicians who are successful train and practice until all the movement on the stage appears to be completely natural.

If something sneaky is going on, it should not look out of place. The sneaky move should look like every other move made during the routine. It should also look like moves people have seen all their lives. The reason is that the brain tends to ignore familiar moves, just as is does small movements.

Technically, tricks that incorporate natural movements can be included under the heading of tricks based on past experience. But this chapter is devoted to tricks that rely very heavily on smooth, natural movements.

If you wish to make a coin vanish by sleight of hand, you must move your hands in a natural manner or the trick won't work. The next trick also relies on a bit of sticky tape.

The Vanishing Coin

Effect:
A coin vanishes from your closed fist.

Props:
- A quarter.

- A 1-inch (2.5-cm) piece of cellophane tape made into a loop with sticky side out.

- A small magic wand, 2 inches (5 cm) in length. You may use a toothpick painted black with white tips.

Setup:
Stick the loop of tape to the back, tails side, of the quarter. The loop of tape should be hidden when looking at the face, or heads side, of the quarter. Place the magic wand in your right pocket.

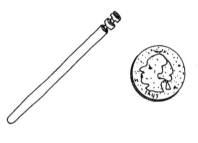

Routine:
Place the quarter, tape-side down, onto your right palm, as shown in Figure 42. The tape should cling to your palm, holding the coin in place. Hold the left hand, palm up, next to your right hand.

Turn your right hand over as in Figure 43, apparently dropping the coin onto your left palm.

The right hand should remain open, with its back to the spectator, appearing to be empty. Close the left hand as if to hold the coin.

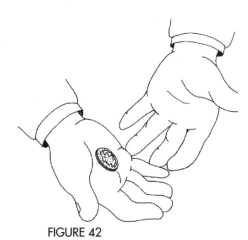

FIGURE 42

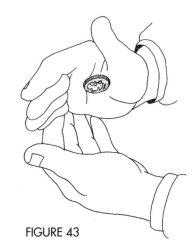

FIGURE 43

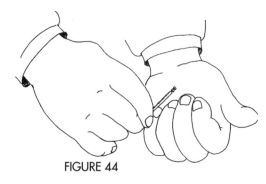

FIGURE 44

Keep the back of the right hand toward the audience. Place your right hand in the pocket that holds the wand. When your hand is inside the pocket, remove the coin and tape from your palm. Pick up the magic wand, and take your hand from your pocket. The coin and tape should be left behind in the pocket.

Wave the wand over the left hand, as in Figure 44. After a few moments, open up the left hand to show that the coin has vanished.

The Perception:

The key to this trick, aside from the tape, is accurately mimicking the move of dropping a coin from one hand to another. If it looks like the move people have seen countless times before, their brains will barely register it.

So the real secret of this trick is to practice until you're fed up and then practice some more. If you wish to fool people, the moves must become second nature to you.

To ensure that the moves look natural, try placing a coin in the palm of your right hand and turning your hand over, dropping the coin onto your left palm. As the coin hits your left palm, close the left hand into a loose fist to hold the coin securely. Observe the actions of both hands as you transfer the coin from one hand to the other.

When you practice the trick with the taped coin, you should mimic these natural actions. If you move or hold your hands in an unnatural way, the audience will suspect something sneaky has happened. And they will be right.

The Finger-Palm

Once you have mastered the previous trick, you might wish to try it with true sleight of hand. To do that, dispense with the tape and hold the coin in "finger-palm position." The finger-palm is easy to explain but difficult to master, because of the importance of looking natural.

FIGURE 45

Hold your right palm up, with your fingers outstretched. Place a quarter at the base of the ring and middle finger, as shown in Figure 45. Then allow your fingers to curl up naturally.

If the coin is placed properly, one edge of the coin will be in contact with the fold of skin between the palm and the fingers, and the opposite edge will nestle in the first joints of the ring and middle fingers.

Turn the right-hand palm toward the floor, adjusting the amount of curl in your fingers so that the coin is lightly held by its edges. If you hold the fingers too tightly, it will look as if you are holding something. If you hold the coin too loosely, it will fall.

Try keeping a coin in finger-palm while watching TV, reading a book, or doing your homework. To do the finger-palm well, it should become as natural as breathing.

Once you have mastered the finger-palm, you can begin working on the coin vanish. Again, first observe the moves you actually make when dropping the coin.

Place the coin on your right fingers, just as if you were going to place it in finger-palm position. Then turn the right hand over and deposit the coin onto the left palm. As the coin hits the left palm curl the fingers of the left hand into a loose fist, hiding the coin from the view of the spectators.

Repeat this move a number of times, observing how your hands move and look before, during, and after the transfer. Now try to duplicate those moves while retaining the coin in the finger-palm position.

Once you have learned to do the fake transfer with the aid of the finger-palm, you can vanish a coin without the loop of tape.

The Bent Spoon

This is one of my favorite tricks, and I do it frequently in restaurants. Once, sitting with some friends, I asked the waitress, "Is this one of those bendable spoons?" I then pretended to bend the spoon.

She screamed, "No! You're not allowed to do that!" I said "O.K. I'm sorry," and proceeded to "straighten" it out. She had a look of wonderful confusion on her face and, realizing it was just a trick, she joined in as we laughed.

Effect:
You bend a spoon and then magically straighten it out. It's more impressive if you use a spoon that just happens to be lying around.

Prop:
  • A spoon—borrowed is better.

Routine:
There are a number of variations on this trick. Each one has a different subtlety, but they all accomplish the same thing. They fool the heck out of anyone watching.

The basic move for this trick is called "the grip." Hold the spoon as shown in Figure 46. The bowl of the spoon should hang from your lower fist, with the spoon exiting the fist between the third and fourth fingers.

From the front, it should appear to the audience that you are simply holding the spoon in what might be called a "power grip." They will think that the thumb of the lower hand is wrapped around the back of the spoon.

But the rear view in Figure 47 shows that the thumb of the lower hand is actually inside the fingers of the upper

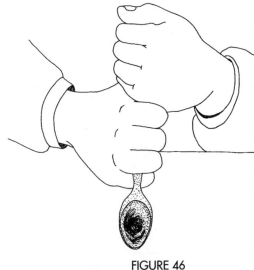

FIGURE 46

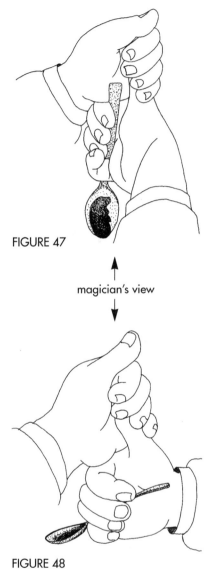

FIGURE 47

↑
magician's view
↓

FIGURE 48

hand. Gripping the thumb in this way keeps your hands aligned, and it will also enhance the illusion that you are actually bending the spoon's handle.

Variation 1
Holding the spoon in the grip, place the tip of the spoon's bowl onto the tabletop. Start to press down. Behind your hands, allow the spoon handle to move away from your fingers. As you do this, your hands should remain upright, just as if they were still holding the handle.

As the handle approaches a horizontal position, the spoon will appear to the spectators to be bending. They will think that the bowl is at a 90° angle to the handle.

When your lower hand reaches the tabletop surface, squeeze the spoon tightly between the third and fourth fingers so that the spoon remains horizontal. Continuing to grip your thumb, slowly lift your hands from the table, as shown in

Figure 48. If this move is done correctly, it should appear that the hands are gripping the handle of a bent spoon.

Hold that position for a count of five.

To "straighten" the spoon, open the fingers of the upper hand wide, and then quickly move the upper hand down to the bowl of the spoon over the back of the lower hand. Push the bowl of the spoon down with your fingers as if you are straightening it. The spoon should pivot on the fingers of your lower hand so that the handle comes back to a vertical position. When the spoon stops pivoting, pick it up and then leave it on the tabletop so that the spectators will see that it is unharmed.

Variation 2

You can enhance the illusion of bending the spoon by placing something in your top hand that looks like the top of the spoon handle. Before putting the spoon in the grip, hide a nickel in the crotch of your upper hand's thumb. Press your thumb tightly against the curled forefinger to hold the nickel flat against the forefinger.

When you are in the grip, let the nickel just barely show. Spectators will think it is the top of the handle sticking out of your upper hand.

Straighten the spoon as before, but take care not to drop the nickel on the tabletop while you are maneuvering the spoon.

Variation 3

The previous variations depend upon visual cues to suggest that the performer is bending the spoon. This version uses an aural, or hearing, cue in addition to a visual one.

You must vary the grip slightly for this version.

Instead of putting the spoon between the fingers of your bottom hand, let it protrude from the bottom of your fist. Then when you "bend" the spoon, allow the handle to smack against the tabletop. This noise will absolutely convince the audience that you have broken the spoon.

To retrieve the spoon, open the upper fingers and bring them down on the bowl. Push on the bowl so that it pivots on the tabletop, bringing the handle to a vertical position. Show the audience that it is unharmed.

The Perception:

These variations on the same trick use different clues to fool the spectator. In the first one, the hands never change position as the bowl of the spoon rotates. This visually simulates what would happen if someone were to actually bend a spoon. It is a natural move.

The second variation takes it one step further. Not only does the spoon bend, but spectators can see some metal at the top of the upper fist. Based on past experience, people assume it is the spoon handle protruding from the top of the upper fist. If there is any doubt that the spoon is being bent, the nickel is a great convincer.

The final version has a convincer of quite another sort. Not only is the visual clue there, but the noise accompanying it startles people and contributes to the illusion.

When people hear the smack of the spoon on the tabletop and see a rapid motion, they assume that something has broken. Strangely enough, if you were really to bend a spoon, the chances of breaking it are very slight. The smacking noise would probably not occur.

The Gypsy Switch

This trick dates back many years, but was first seen in print in a magazine called *Kabbalah,* edited by John Racherbaumer. The moves seem to take forever to explain in writing, but the whole trick takes only seconds to perform. Try it and you will see how easily you can fool your friends.

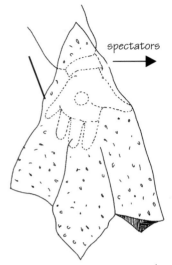

FIGURE 49

Effect:

A borrowed coin, placed in the center of a bandanna, changes into a stone.

Props:

• A clean bandanna.

• A smooth, circular stone about the size of a quarter.

Setup:

The bandanna should be folded and placed in your pocket. The stone should be easily accessible to your left hand.

FIGURE 50

Routine:

Casually take the stone into your left hand in finger-palm position (see page 62). Hold your hand as loose and natural as possible so no one will suspect that there is anything in it.

Open up the bandanna and place it over your left palm. As you do this, let the stone flop over into the center of your palm. It should now be covered by

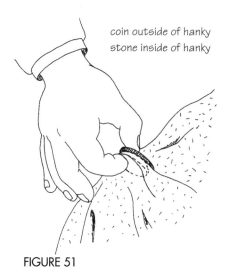

coin outside of hanky
stone inside of hanky

FIGURE 51

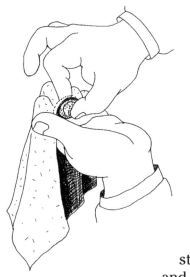

FIGURE 52

the bandanna, as shown in Figure 49.

Ask someone to loan you a quarter. When you get one, place it on the bandanna directly on top of the stone, as shown in Figure 50. The left hand, with palm facing up, should be opened wide with the left thumb pointing toward the spectator.

Bring your right hand over the left hand and place the right thumb on top of the borrowed quarter. Put your right index finger down on the bandanna in front of the coin and pinch the stone underneath with your thumb. You should now be pinching the quarter, the bandanna, and the stone between the thumb and forefinger, as shown in Figure 51.

Moving everything upward and forward toward the spectator, drag the bandanna off the left palm. As you take the bandanna from the left palm, turn the right hand slightly so that the bandanna hides the view of the quarter from the spectator.

When the bandanna clears the left palm, place the quarter, bandanna, and stone on the left palm, letting the rest of the bandanna drape over the front of the hand, as shown in Figure 52. As you do this, secretly put the quarter into finger-palm position.

Gently curl your left hand around the bandanna and the stone. With the right hand, grasp the free ends of the bandanna hanging from the left hand and pull the bandanna from the left fist, leaving the quarter in finger-palm.

As the center of the bandanna swings free of the left fist, the weight of the stone will pull it down, just as if you had the quarter inside the handkerchief. The audience will think that the quarter is inside.

Let the left fist holding the quarter fall naturally to your side and hand the bandanna to a spectator.

Reach into your pocket with your left hand to get out a bit of "invisible magic woofle dust," and leave the quarter behind. Sprinkle the woofle dust over the bandanna. Ask your spectator to open the bandanna and take the quarter out. The audience will be pretty darn surprised to find that the quarter has changed into a stone.

The Perception:
Once again natural moves come into play. When the spectator watches you perform this trick, he will assume that you have simply wrapped the quarter in the bandanna. That's the appearance.

If you examine the moves carefully, you will find that the quarter never gets wrapped inside the bandanna. Your bold, straightforward moves, plus the weight of the stone, will make the spectator believe that you have fairly wrapped the coin in the bandanna.

I've Got Your Card on My Mind

The sneaky move in this trick was originated by U.F. Grant in the 1940s.

Effect:

While trying to guess a card chosen by a spectator, the performer seems to have lost it in the deck, but then finds it in a humorous manner.

Prop:

• A deck of cards.

Setup:

Turn one card upside down on the bottom of the deck. Place the deck face down in your left hand.

Routine:

With both palms up, spread the cards slowly from your left hand into your right hand. You should see only the backs of the cards. Make sure the spectator does not see the reversed card on the bottom of the deck.

As you spread them, have the spectator choose and remove a card from the deck. Ask him to look at it and remember it. Then square up the deck in the left hand and have the spectator place the selection on top of the deck.

Cut the deck in half and place the bottom half on top of the other half. The selected card should now be in the center of the deck underneath the reversed card.

Say something to the effect of, "Your card is lost in the middle of the deck." Begin spreading the cards from the top of the deck into the right hand, saying, "Neither one of us knows where your card is."

When you come across the reversed card, as

shown in Figure 53, act surprised and say, "This isn't
your card, is it?" The spectator should agree that it is
not his.

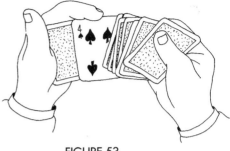

FIGURE 53

Put the reversed card
on the bottom of the
packet in your right hand,
as in Figure 54. Don't
move the left hand. Now
with your right fingertips
against the reversed card,
grip the cards in the right
hand firmly and turn it
palm down. The reversed
card should now be on
top and the rest of the
cards on bottom.

Nonchalantly trans-
fer the single face-down
card that is now on top of
the right-hand packet
onto the bottom of the
left-hand packet, as shown
in Figure 55. Turn the

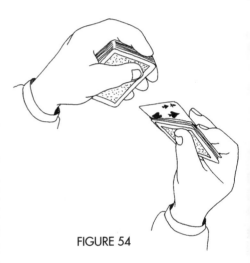

FIGURE 54

right-hand packet back to the palm-up position, as in
Figure 56. Place the cards in the right hand, now face
down, under the cards in the left hand. Square up the
deck.

You should now hold the entire face-down deck
in the left hand. What you have done is secretly bring
the selected card to the top of the deck through a set
of openly visible maneuvers.

Holding the face-down deck in your left hand, say,
"I want you to think of your card. I'm trying to get a
mental impression of it." Bring your left hand to your

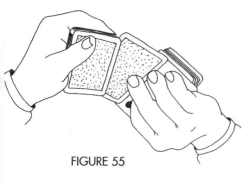

FIGURE 55

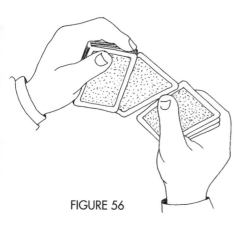

FIGURE 56

FIGURE 57

forehead so that the top (selected card) touches your skin.

Then say, "I'm getting an impression of the card." As you say this, slowly drag the deck across your forehead, as shown in Figure 57. The friction between the top card and your skin should make the top card stay in place as the other cards move down. The spectator will be rather surpised to see that the card he chose is the one "on your mind."

The Perception:

When they see the face-up card, the audience thinks you have messed up the trick. It is actually a marker for the selected card, but since you put it on the bottom of the deck naturally as you did the rest of the cards, the audience suspects nothing.

Turning the right hand over and back also seems like part of the natural moves a card dealer would make to right the reversed card. They keep the audience's mind off the cards in the left hand, where the selected card sits at the top the whole time. If you practice these moves until you can do them smoothly, the card manipulations will fool the most astute of observers.

The Inside-Out Card Warp

The idea for this trick originated with the magician Jeff Busby. It fools the audience with the help of a simple rip in a playing card.

Effect:

A playing card turns inside out.

Props:

  • Two playing cards.

Setup:

Rip one card halfway through its width, starting from the center of a long side, as shown in Figure 58. Place both cards together in a pocket or other easily accessible place. It also helps to have a tabletop or other surface in front of you.

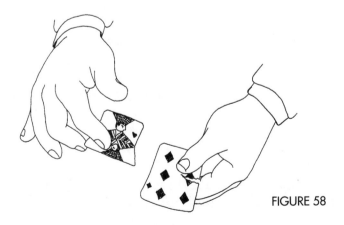

FIGURE 58

Routine:
Take the two cards out of your pocket and hold them in your left hand. The unripped card should be on top, covering the ripped card. As you slide the top card into your right hand, move your left thumb over the rip in the other card, concealing the tear from the audience. Hand the unripped card to a spectator.

Using your left fingers to cover the rip, fold your card in half lengthwise, as shown in Figure 59, so that the long edges meet.

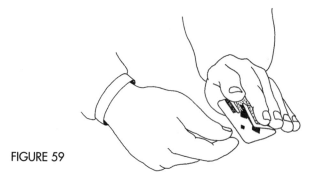

FIGURE 59

Ask the spectator to crease her card, folding it in half widthwise, so that the short edges meet. Then have her open the card flat. Making sure that the ripped half of your card is folded underneath the other half, display the folded card on your open left palm.

Take the card from the spectator and align the folded edge of your card with the crease on the face of the spectator's card. Holding both cards by your right fingertips, slide the ripped card to the left with your left fingers until the right edges of the cards are aligned.

Slide your right thumb along the inside crease of the ripped card until it is just to the right of the rip.

Grasp both cards between the right thumb and fingertips, keeping the back of the unripped card toward the spectator.

Pinch the left edge of the ripped card closed with your left fingertips and rotate it upward 180 degrees, as shown in Figure 60. The right-hand portion of the ripped card should be opened flat against the other card, while the left side is folded with both edges up, as in Figure 61.

Now say, "I am going to take you on a trip to the land of the impossible. To enter this twilight zone of magic, all we have to do is make a left turn with this card."

Hold the bottom flap

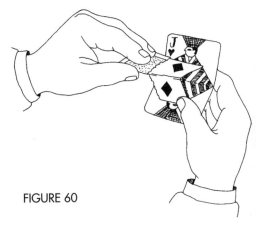

FIGURE 60

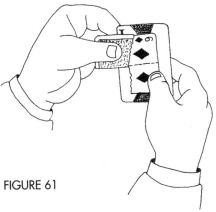

FIGURE 61

of the ripped card firmly against the unripped card with your right thumb. Now twist the left side of the ripped card forward an additional 180 degrees, while letting the right side of the card fold in half in a direction opposite to the original fold.

It requires a lot of practice to learn the proper touch for this move. The right side of the card must be held loosely enough so that the left side can twist around, but tightly enough so that it doesn't fly out of control and reveal the rip.

FIGURE 62

You should end up with a card that is half face-out and half face-in as shown in Figure 62. The crease of the ripped card should be touching the crease of the unripped card.

The audience will think that all you did was turn the folded card over. The back of the unripped card should cover everything.

Fold the unripped card in half as before, sandwiching the ripped card in the center. The back-out half of the ripped card should stick out from the left side of the sandwich.

Hold the outer card at the lower edges between the thumb and first finger of the right hand. With your left index finger, push the ripped card quickly through the sandwich until the right half sticks out of the right side of the sandwich. Don't push it so far that the rip shows.

Since the face side of the card is out on the right half, it will look to the spectator as if the card turned inside out. Turn your hand over so that the spectators can see that the sandwiched card is face-out on both sides.

Push the card back through the sandwich from the right side to show the other half. Once again turn your hand over to display both sides. Just to make sure there is no question of your powers, repeat the push-through one more time.

Now to get out of the trick gracefully, leaving behind no evidence of your method, hold the sandwich with your right fingers. Grasp the right edge of the sandwich from above between the left first finger and

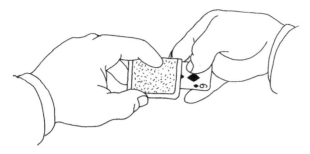

FIGURE 63

thumb, placing the finger along the edge facing the spectators. Slide the inside card out of the sandwich, as shown in Figure 63, until you see the rip, but conceal it from the spectators with your left forefinger.

With your right hand, rip the inside card in half, completing the rip already begun, and drop the right half on the tabletop. The audience should see a face-out half-card. Release the pressure of the left fingers and allow the back-out half-card to fall to the tabletop.

Open up the sandwich and display it to the audience. Then drop it onto the tabletop away from the two halves.

Open up both halves and arrange them so that they are face up. Align the ripped edges. The perfect matching of the rips will convince the spectators that you used only one card.

The Perception:
This trick is made up of a series of small moves that must look natural. You must first of all hide the rip in the card without arousing suspicion. You may be able to simply pinch the card together at its edge to keep the audience from perceiving the rip. It helps to use a picture card for the ripped card because the printing on it will camouflage the rip.

Even though the card in front conceals much of

what you are doing from the audience, the way you manipulate the ripped card is important. Your movements must be so smooth and natural that the audience perceives them as turning the card over.

CONFUSING THE SENSES

There are a number of tricks that present stimuli or sense data in a manner that confuses the senses. Although the next trick hinges on making natural movements, it includes an optical illusion that rearranges impulses to the brain. The brain's erroneous interpretation of these impulses gives the trick a nice twist.

The trick also works on the basis of another secret weapon that magicians rely on: cheating and lying. Of course, we magicians prefer to call it mental deception.

My patter often includes something along these lines:

"There are two types of people who always lie. The first is magicians, and the second is politicians. It's really hard to trust either group, but all in all I think magicians are more honest because they always let you know they're lying."

The X-Ray Tube

Effect:
A spectator picks a card and hides it in his hand. With the aid of a simple cardboard tube, you "x-ray" the spectator's hand and announce the card behind it.

Props:
  • A deck of cards.

- An empty cardboard tube from the center of a roll of paper towel or bathroom tissue.

The Illusion:

The "x-raying" of a hand is not such a difficult feat if you take advantage of a well-known optical illusion. Hold the paper tube like a telescope in your right hand, as shown in Figure 64. Place it carefully against your right eye so that you can see out the other end of the tube.

FIGURE 64

Open your left hand flat and vertical, with the palm toward you. Place the blade (the edge of the hand beneath the pinky) next to the paper tube, about 3 inches (about 8 cm) from your left eye.

With both eyes open, you should see a pretty cool illusion. It should look as if there is a hole in your hand, as shown in Figure 65. The illusion comes about as a result of the way your brain interprets the sense data coming from your eyes.

FIGURE 65

Ordinarily both eyes focus on the same object or scene. But each eye sends a separate image to the brain, and the brain learns to form the two images into one. It interprets the images assuming that they are only slightly different from each other.

In this case, however, the views are very different because of the cardboard tube. The right eye sees the view through the tube, while the left eye sees the palm of the left hand. Your brain combines these two images as best it can to give you one image. As a result, you get the illusion of a hole in your hand.

You can use this illusion to make the spectator believe that the tube lets you see right through her hand.

Routine:

In this trick, you won't have to find out what card the audience member selects because you will already know it. All you have to do is trick the spectator into taking a card you have already seen. Magicians call this "forcing" a card on the spectator.

My favorite method is the crisscross force. Say you want to force the three of diamonds. Make sure the three of diamonds is on top of the deck and put the deck on the table. Have the spectator cut the deck in half and place the top half next to the bottom half on the table.

Then lay the bottom half on the top half so that they are crisscrossed. At this point, show the spectator how the tube creates a hole in his hand. Now remove the half of the deck on top (formerly, the bottom half) and ask the spectator to turn over the top card on the remaining half.

Here's where the trickery comes in. When you make the request, say:

"Please take the card that you cut to. Don't even look at it. Place it face down on your left palm. Now cover the card with your right palm so that it is sandwiched between your hands. Neither you nor I know the card, but I'm going to use my x-ray tube to identify your card."

Unless the spectator is very observant, he should not notice that you have made him think the top half of the deck is the bottom half. Put the back of the tube against one of his hands. Look through it and make believe you are focusing it by twisting it back and forth.

Now say:

"I see a red card. It's a little blurry. Let me focus this thing better. It's a diamond. A three of diamonds. Would you please open your hands and verify the card?"

The Perception:

The natural move here is placing the bottom half of the deck on the top half after the spectator has cut it. The audience thinks that you are simply marking the cut by placing it on top. In reality, you are marking the card that you want to force them to select.

Things happen too smoothly and quickly for the spectator to realize what is going on. Showing the x-ray tube in the middle of all of this also occupies the brain to help distract it from what is going on.

Of course, your "verbal deceptions" help point the brain in the direction you want to go. We'll have more fun with verbal deceptions in the next chapter.

SOUND
AND TOUCH

A s Professor Baumrin pointed out, people don't respond to deception based on sound and touch as well as they do to visual deception. But when the performer manipulates these other two senses in addition to our visual perception, the effect can be quite impressive.

Ventriloquists probably know more about hearing deception than any other performer. Besides keeping their lips from moving, ventriloquists use other visual cues to make the audience believe that the dummy is talking. The dummy's mouth moves, as well as its eyes and head. The ventriloquist controls the movements with levers inside the dummy's body.

Also very important is the fact that ventriloquists talk to their dummy as if it is a live person, looking directly at it. Sometimes the effect is so skillfully done that the dummy seems to come alive.

Gary Willner, a world renowned ventriloquist, has a most unusual "vent act." He uses life-size dummies that look exactly like Frank Sinatra, Elvis Presley, and Nat King Cole.

Ventriloquist Gary Willner uses many visual cues in addition to creating his dummy's voice in order to fool the audience.

He worked for years to get the voices down to perfection. As a result, he sounds exactly like them when he sings even though he's not moving his lips. Not only that, but he has practiced the body movements so well that his dummies look more alive than a lot of people.

Another well-known vent act in the United States is Dan Ritchard and Conrad Burdee. Dan is a master ventriloquist. I am always amazed how he has gotten the "telephone voice" down to perfection. He can

Ventriloquist Dan Ritchard, shown with Conrad Burdee, is a master at holding make-believe phone conversations.

pick up any phone and hold a make-believe conversation that convinces eavesdroppers he is on the line with someone.

Besides saying all the right things, Dan does all of the body movements, such as nodding and grimacing that we all do when making a phone call. As a gag, he will often pick up a public pay phone and hold a ridiculous conversation with a nonexistent someone on the other end.

In the next trick, you'll find out how ventriloquists "throw" their voices.

The Mystical Marble

Effect:
A marble trapped between two pie plates acts in a peculiar manner.

Props:
- A marble.

- Two aluminum (not aluminum foil) pie plates.

- A small metal thimble painted the same color as your skin.

- A deck of cards.

Setup:
The thimble and cards should be in an easily accessible pocket. The pie plates and marble should be on a table in front of you.

Routine:
Explain to your spectators that the marble is actually a small crystal ball and can reveal secrets. Place the marble in one pie plate. Turn the second pie plate upside down and cover the first. They should now be mouth to mouth, with the marble in the center.

Force a card on your friend using the crisscross force (See p. 81). Put the deck back in your pocket. As your hand goes in the pocket, slip the thimble on your middle fingertip. Bring your hand from the pocket, slightly curved, in a natural position.

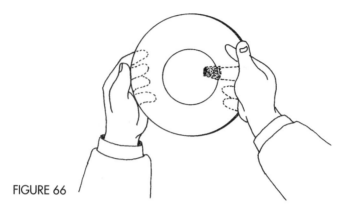

FIGURE 66

Pay no attention to the hand with the thimble and the spectators will not even know the thimble is there. If you don't think it's worth looking at, neither will they.

Pick up the pie plates as in Figure 66, thumbs on top, fingers below. Keep the bottom of the lower plate below the lines of sight of the spectators.

Then say, "The miniature crystal ball inside the pie plates can answer questions by tapping out answers. It will tap once for yes and twice for no. Let's try it out."

Have one of your friends ask a question of the crystal ball that can be answered yes or no. It will help if you have them ask questions that you know the answer to, such as: "Is my name ___?" "Do I have red hair?"

You then tap out the answer with the thimble on your finger. Tap once for yes and twice for no. It takes some practice to tap the bottom of the pie plate with as little movement as possible while tapping as loudly as possible. If you practice a bit beforehand, you should have no problem getting the hang of it.

Now ask the crystal ball, "Is the selected card a red card?"

Tap the right answer. Remember that you forced the card, so you already know the answer.

Then ask, "Is it a number card?"

Then, "Is it the six of clubs?"

It works best to limit yourself to three or four questions. When the "crystal ball" has correctly identified the card, place the pie plates on the table-top and ask a spectator to examine the plates and the crystal ball.

While the examination is taking place, take the deck of cards out of your pocket. As you reach in to take the deck of cards, leave the thimble behind. Now everything—the card, the pie plates, and the marble—may be examined.

The Perception:

It is impossible for the human ear to recognize where the tapping sound is coming from. Is it inside the pie plate or outside? The spectators will hear the same sound from either location.

The thimble can't be seen for three reasons. It is camouflaged by the skin-colored paint, and it is hidden beneath the bottom of the pie plate. Finally, by acting cool when you put the thimble on, you arouse no suspicions.

You also relied on the old verbal deception, by saying that the crystal ball was going to do the tapping. Once you lead the audience down the garden path with a story, it is hard for them to get it out of their minds. People will actually think you have a remote-controlled marble before they will think you are making the noise on the outside of the pie plate.

Another reason they assume the noise is coming from the inside is that the audience looks where you look. If you look at the middle of the pie plates, the audience does too. This is the same device a ventriloquist uses to make it seem that the voice is coming from the dummy.

From experience, people know that other people look in the direction of a noise. Since you are closer to the pie plate, they assume without even thinking about it that you can pinpoint the direction of the noise better than they.

The Coin That Wasn't There
This trick confuses the sense of touch in much the same way that the x-ray tube on p. 79 fools the sense of sight.

Effect:
With her eyes closed, the spectator feels two coins underneath her fingertips. When she opens them, she finds that the magician has made one coin vanish.

Prop:
• A quarter.

Routine:
Have your spectator cross the first and second fingers of her right hand and shut her eyes. Take the quarter out of your pocket and tell her, "I'm going to put two quarters at your fingertips."

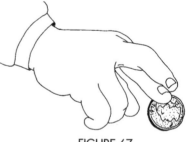

FIGURE 67

This is a fib because you will put only one quarter underneath her two fingertips as shown in Figure 67.

Ask, "How many do you feel?"

She should answer, "Two."

Now tell her that you will make one of them disappear by magic. Snap the fingers of your free hand and ask her to open her eyes. She will undoubtedly be surprised to find only one coin under her finger.

The Perception:

We have learned from experience to recognize objects based on what our fingers feel. We can tell how many coins are underneath our fingers with no problem—at least when our fingers are not crossed.

Crossing the fingers confuses the brain. Even though the fingers are touching only one object, the brain tells us there are two because it is receiving data from two sensory inputs (our fingers) on the skin that are not in their normal positions. When the eyes open, our sense of vision corrects the mistake our sense of touch makes.

It is very difficult to perform this illusion on yourself because you know what is really there. I know because I tried it on myself a number of times when I first read about the trick, which has been written up in magic books for well over one hundred years.

These older books usually say to put a marble instead of a coin under crossed fingers. This was supposed to feel like two marbles, but after trying it a number of times, I still didn't know what they were talking about. I'm grateful to the magician and toy designer Mark Setteducati for showing me how this trick works.

THE POWER OF SUGGESTION

These next few items are gags more than magic tricks. I call them "cool tricks to gross your friends out." They depend very heavily on verbal deception, or the power of suggestion, and are augmented by sound and touch cues.

The Flick

Effect:
A wise guy pulls a piece of indeterminate flotsam from his soft drink cup and flings it at a horrified dinner companion.

Props:
• A small paper square, 1/2 inch by 1/2 inch (about 1 cm by 1 cm).

• A drink, preferably ordered at a restaurant.

Setup:
Wad the paper square into a small ball. Put the ball on the pad of the right thumb. As shown in Figure 68, position the middle fingernail of the right hand against the paper ball, in such a way that you can readily flick it across the room.

This gag works best using a soft drink you've gotten at a fast-food restaurant, but any drink will do.

FIGURE 68

Routine:
After sipping from your drink, point into it with your right index finger as though something were inside. Reach into the cup with your right index finger and

pretend that you have picked out a distasteful object and that you're going to flick it at your friend. Flick the paper ball instead, as shown in Figure 69.

FIGURE 69

The Perception:
The principle operating here is visual deception, aided by touch deception. By pointing into the cup with a look of dismay, you make your friends believe there is something awful floating in it. You continue the hoax by pretending to pull it out. When your victim feels the paper wad on his skin, he no longer has any doubt that you have pulled something nasty out of your cup.

The gag also relies to some extent on a large movement masking a small movement. The movement of your hand coming out of the cup distracts from the small flick of your middle finger. This trick should convince your friends that you are a truly disgusting person.

The Sneeze

Effect:
A yucky human sneezes, spraying a person sitting across the table.

Prop:
• A glass of water.

Setup:

You should be sitting at a table with at least one person, eating or just talking, with the glass of water nearby. When no one is looking, wet the fingertips of one hand thoroughly.

Routine:

As you sit across the table from someone, act as if you are going to sneeze. Put one hand under the nose, then the other. Keep your hand near your face.

After a few moments, fake a sneeze. When people sneeze, the upper body often rocks back and forth, so include that motion. At the same time, discreetly flick your fingers in the direction of your victim, getting him all wet.

The Perception:

Just as in the last gag, visual and touch deception plays the major role, and small-movement-masked-by-a-large-movement plays a supporting role.

You fool the victim into thinking you've sneezed

by making all the right moves, and by simulating the feeling stimuli involved when a sneeze sprays on bystanders. The rocking motion and the movement of your arms makes the flicking of your water-soaked fingers difficult to perceive.

If properly orchestrated, all of these factors should lead your victim to believe that your hygiene habits leave much to be desired.

The Egghead Massage

Effect:
A master of torture breaks a raw egg over the head of a victim and then makes the egg vanish.

Prop:
• A hard-boiled egg.

Routine:
Have a friend sit down on a chair at a table. Take the egg from your pocket and place it on the table. Step behind the chair and pick up the egg. Tell your friend that you will demonstrate how to make the egg disappear, but that in order to do so, he must keep looking straight ahead.

Put the egg in your pocket. Ready your hands, as shown in Figure 70. Say, "First I have to break the egg," and gently tap the top of your friend's head, as though cracking the egg.

Spread your fingers wide apart and gently touch your friends hair, as shown in Figure 71. Slowly move your fingers downward, barely contacting the hair.

If you do this with just the right touch, your friend will get the creepy feeling that you've broken an egg on his head. After the egg has covered his head and neck, say, "Now to make it disappear."

FIGURE 70

Take your hands away from the hair and allow your friend to touch it with his fingers. He will be amazed to find that his hair is not a gooey mess.

The Perception:

We normally don't think of our hair and scalp as being parts of a sense organ. Touching the hair even gently moves the scalp, sending touch impulses to the brain. The sensation is weird, almost like a tickling feeling. It will not occur if you touch too much hair at once or if you apply too much pressure.

Because the feeling is difficult to identify, it is easy for your friend to assume that it could be just like the feeling of a raw egg oozing down the scalp.

FIGURE 71

If you want to experiment with the sensation, get in the shower and let some shampoo drip from the bottle directly onto your dry hair. As the shampoo drips down your scalp in tiny streams, you should get a spooky feeling. Notice that if you put the shampoo on your palm and then rub it on, you don't get the tickling feeling because you feel pressure all over your scalp.

My theory is that it is the same feeling cats get when their whiskers brush against an object as they are stalking in the dark. A tingling sensation warns them that something is there.

The Great Crackup

Effect:
A weird person twists his neck with his hands, creating an awful cracking sound that freaks out bystanders.

Prop:
- A small polystyrene plastic cup, about the size of a shot glass. If it's not available, you can substitute empty Tic-Tac® mint boxes.

Routine:
Hold the cup loosely in your right hand. Don't let anyone see it, but don't make any noticeable effort to conceal it either.

Say to someone nearby, "My neck has really been bothering me. I'm going to try to crack it."

Act as if you are going to twist your head from left to right by placing your right hand near the back of your head and your left hand at your chin as in Figure 72. As you pretend to twist your head, crack the cup with your fingertips. People will assume that you have indeed cracked your neck.

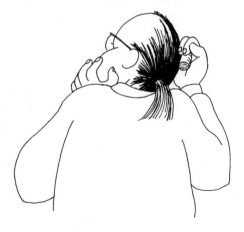

FIGURE 72

The Perception:

This gag works on the basis of verbal and visual deception enhanced by sound cues. It also relies a great deal on past experience.

There is probably no one alive who has not seen and heard someone cracking their knuckles. So when people hear a similar but louder noise while you are manipulating your head, they can't help but think your neck is cracking and that you need help—if not medical help, then mental help!

How to Remove a Finger

Effect:

A bumbling idiot cracks a knuckle so loudly that bystanders think the finger may be broken.

Props:

•   Your fingers.

Routine:

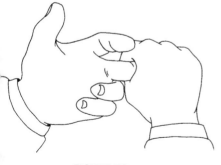

FIGURE 73

Extend all the fingers of your left hand and make a loose fist with your right hand. Insert the second finger of your left hand into the hole in your right fist formed by the thumb and first finger, as shown in Figure 73.

Before actually pulling this prank, you must practice

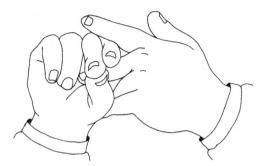

FIGURE 74

snapping the fingers of your right hand while they are around the second finger of the left hand, as shown in Figure 74. You can get a very loud and convincing snap if you practice enough.

Now with your left palm up, bend the free fingers of your left hand upward so that they form a right angle with the left palm. The right fist should continue to hold the left second finger.

> You must take care to do the next motion gently so that you don't hurt yourself.

Pretend to pull the left second finger downward with the right fist, and snap your right fingers at the same time. Bystanders will think that you have seriously cracked your second finger knuckle. If you grimace well enough, some might even think you broke your finger.

The Perception:
Again, we rely here on the fact

that much of people's perception comes from past experience. We all know how it looks and sounds when people crack their knuckles. When we get visual and hearing sensations that are very close to what we've seen before, we assume that the same thing must be happening.

FOR FURTHER READING

Bobo, J. B. *Modern Coin Magic.* Minneapolis: C. W. Jones, 1952.

Churchill, E. Richard. *How to Make Optical Illusion Tricks and Toys.* New York: Sterling, 1989.

Gardner, Robert. *Experimenting With Illusions.* New York: Franklin Watts, 1990.

Goldston, Will. *Exclusive Magical Secrets.* New York: Dover Publications, 1977.

Hoffmann, Prof. *Hoffmann's Modern Magic.* New York: Dover, 1978 (reprint).

Lukiesch, M. *Visual Illusion.* New York: Dover, 1965.

Ritchard, Dan. *Ventriloquism for the Total Dummy.* New York: Villard Books, 1987.

White, Larry and Ray Broekel. *A First Book of Optical Illusion.* New York: Franklin Watts, 1986.

RESOURCES

Suppliers of Magical Apparatus
The following companies will send you their catalogs and other information for free. Just asked to be put on their mailing lists and include a stamped, self-addressed no. 10 (or larger) envelope with your request.

Abbott's Magic Co.
Colon, MI 49040

The Studio
P.O. Box 8486
Metairie, LA 70011

Hank Lee's Magic Factory
125 Lincoln Street
Boston, MA 02205

Show-Biz Services
1735 East 26th Street
Brooklyn, NY 11229

Louis Tannen, Inc.
6 West 32nd Street
New York, NY 10001–3808

Zanadu
772 Newark Avenue
Jersey City, NJ 07306

Magic Magazines
Genii
P. O. Box 36068
Los Angeles, CA 90036

Tops Magic Magazine
c/o Abbott's Magic Co.
Colon, MI 49040

Magic Clubs
International Brotherhood of Magicians
P. O. Box 192090
St. Louis, MO 63119

Society of American Magicians
Young Members
P. O. Box 510260
St. Louis, MO 63151

INDEX

Small movement-masked-by-a-large-movement princi-ple, 36–37, 42, 44, 45, 47, 95, 96
Smell, 12, 14, 16
Sneeze gag, the, 95–96
Sound deceptions, 99, 100. *See also* Hearing decep-tions, verbal deceptions
Stagecraft, 11
Stereoscopic vision, 24–25, 83
Stimuli. *See* Sense data

Taste, 12, 14
Thread, 30–35
Tomlin, Lily, 18
Touch, 13, 14, 86, 92–93, 94, 95, 96–99

Touch deceptions, 95

Vanishing coin trick, the, 63–65, 66
Vanishing paper squares trick, the, 37–41
Ventriloquists, 86–89, 92
Verbal deceptions, 85, 91, 93, 100
Visual deceptions, 86, 95, 96, 100. *See also* Sight de-ceptions

Wand through the head trick, the, 56–58
Willner, Gary, 86, *87*

X-ray tube trick, the, 25, 82–85, 92

ABOUT THE AUTHOR

Bob Friedhoffer has been performing magic tricks for youngsters for almost 30 years. He has written many books for Watts, including *Toying Around With Science: The Physics Behind Toys and Gags* and six books in the Scientific Magic series. His *Magic Tricks, Science Facts* and *More Magic Tricks, Science Facts* were named to the list of best children's science books by *Science Books and Films*.